Copyright © 2023 by Dr Nihara Krause MBE.

All rights reserved. No part of this publication may be reproduced, distributed, or transmitted in any form or by any means, including photocopying, recording, or other electronic or mechanical methods, without the prior written permission of the publisher or author, except in the case of brief quotations embodied in critical reviews and certain other noncommercial uses permitted by copyright law. For permission requests, write to enquiries@stem4.org.uk.

This publication is designed to provide accurate and authoritative information in regard to the subject matter covered. It is sold with the understanding that neither the author nor the publisher is engaged in rendering professional services. While the publisher and author have used their best efforts in preparing this book, they make no representations or warranties with respect to the accuracy or completeness of the contents of this book and specifically disclaim any implied warranties of merchantability or fitness for a particular purpose. The advice and strategies contained herein may not be suitable for your situation. You should consult with a professional when appropriate. Neither the publisher nor the author shall be liable for any loss of profit or any other commercial damages, including but not limited to special, incidental, consequential, personal, or other damages.

ISBN: 9798861403948

www.stem4.org.uk

# INTRODUCTION

Welcome to 'Worried about going to school?' for students in secondary schools and colleges. This is a workbook that will guide a young person through steps they can take to help reduce difficulties around going to school or college, as well as provide signposts for further help.

Sometimes going to school or college can become tough and this can make every day a challenge. Parents, carers, and teachers (and even the young person experiencing it) might have a hard time trying to understand why this has become so difficult.

By working through this booklet, the blocks to getting to school or college may become clear. So that together, and with some of the activities in the Clear Fear app, a young person will hopefully be able to attend school or college, with practice, one step at a time. There are also some suggestions on steps that can be taken to get further support and help.

Everything is a learning process, especially recovery from anxiety or worry. Taking one small step at a time will allow you to take control and start moving forward. Focus on the present and make this your time to leave behind the past so you can get to your future.

**Dr Nihara Krause MBE**
Consultant Clinical Psychologist
CEO and Founder of stem4

---

stem4 is a charity based in London that promotes positive mental health in teenagers. It aims to raise early awareness and highlights the importance of early intervention in teenage mental health issues.

Clear Fear is an app developed for teenage mental health charity stem4 by Dr Nihara Krause MBE, Consultant Clinical Psychologist, and uses the evidence-based treatment Cognitive Behavioural Therapy (CBT) to focus on learning to reduce the physical responses to threat by learning to breathe, relax, and be mindful, as well as changing thoughts and behaviours and releasing emotions.

# CONTENTS

### Exercise 1
Working out why you might be finding it difficult to go to school/college ...... 6

### Exercise 2
Thinking about how you can make going to school/college easier ............ 8

### Exercise 3
Learning to manage your worries and fears ........................................... 14

The circular link between over worry, avoidance, and further worry .......... 14

The negative circle of avoidance ........................................................... 15

What help will usually focus on ............................................................. 15

### Some quick and effective tips to help young people learn to manage their worries and fears ................................... 16

1. Follow the breathing activity on the Clear Fear app if you have it .......... 16
2. Have a break from worrying ............................................................. 18
3. Still feeling tense? Manage your physical responses to anxiety ............ 25
4. Make an action plan with small steps ................................................ 26
5. Keep a happy journal ....................................................................... 28
6. Try Dr Krause's toothbrush thought exercise ..................................... 29

### Wise words on school/college worry ................................. 32

### Parents and carers ............................................................. 33

### Schools and colleges ......................................................... 36

### About stem4 ..................................................................... 40
Who we are .......................................................................................... 40

Dr. Nihara Krause ................................................................................. 41

### Clear Fear ......................................................................... 42

### stem4's mental health apps ............................................. 43

### Signposts for young people ............................................. 44

### Signposts for adults ......................................................... 45

# EXERCISE 1
## Working out why you might be finding it difficult to go to school/college

Whilst worrying is common, sometimes worries become so overwhelming that they can stop a young person from getting on with what they need to, or want to do. This can also apply to attending school or college, leading to what's called Emotionally Based School Avoidance (EBSA).

Sometimes it's hard to know the root of a young person's worries but it's generally useful to find out, so that something can be done to change it.

**Circle any of the reasons below that might apply to you. Be as honest as you can. It's to help explore possible contributory factors**

1. I have fallen out of the routine of school/college after the pandemic
2. I am worried about assessments/exams
3. I find it hard to make or maintain friendships
4. I feel on my own / lonely
5. I worry about my family when I'm at school and wish I was with them
6. I struggle with noise or crowds
7. I'm struggling with some of the work
8. I feel too much of a pressure to achieve
9. I'm not getting on with some of the teachers
10. I find it hard to agree with or follow school rules
11. I find leaving the house difficult
12. I find the journey to school/college and back difficult
13. I don't fit in
14. I'm dealing with a lot of emotional stuff now and can't focus at school/college
15. Some difficult experiences that have happened have left me feeling worried and anxious and it's hard to get over them
16. I'm left out/picked on
17. I experience physical symptoms of anxiety or panic at school that I want to avoid
18. Someone close to me is ill or needs looking after
19. I've lost someone close to me and am finding it hard
20. Any other reason…

*Share these reasons with a trusted adult so that they can see what help you need, and work out the steps to getting back on track.*

## EXERCISE 2
### Thinking about how you can make going to school/college easier

Make yourself comfortable and try to answer the following questions. Be open in your answers, the aim of this exercise is to help identify possible strengths.

**What three things do you like at school/college?**
*For example, you might like a specific subject, or enjoy break time with a friend.*

## What would make going to school/college better?

*For example, it might be easier to avoid travelling in the rush hour or to meet a teacher you feel comfortable with at the school gate, or know you can spend breaks or lunchtime in a safe space.*

**How could you use these ideas to help you face going back to school or college, bit by bit? (You can brainstorm some ideas with someone, if you like)**

*For example, you might aim to go in when your favourite subject is on the timetable and you might try and arrange for the teacher you are comfortable with to take you part-way to the lesson.*

**How positive might you feel about yourself if you were able to face your fear, one small step at a time?**

*For example, you might feel really brave.*

*Share these with a trusted adult so that they can work with you to help you make school/college an easier place for you to be at.*

**Set yourself a promise to get back to school or college, reminding yourself of the positives you will feel in yourself**

*For example, you might say 'I aim to go back to school or college so that I do something brave and feel more confident in myself'.*

**What words or phrases of encouragement could you say to yourself to make sure you can succeed in getting to school?**

*For example, 'I can do it' or 'Without hardship, nothing changes'.*

## EXERCISE 3
### Learning to manage your worries and fears

Getting worried and feeling fearful are perfectly acceptable feelings to have. However, when we get over-worried, feelings intensify and affect our behaviour in many ways. One such behaviour is avoidance, where we try to avoid the thing we are fearful of.

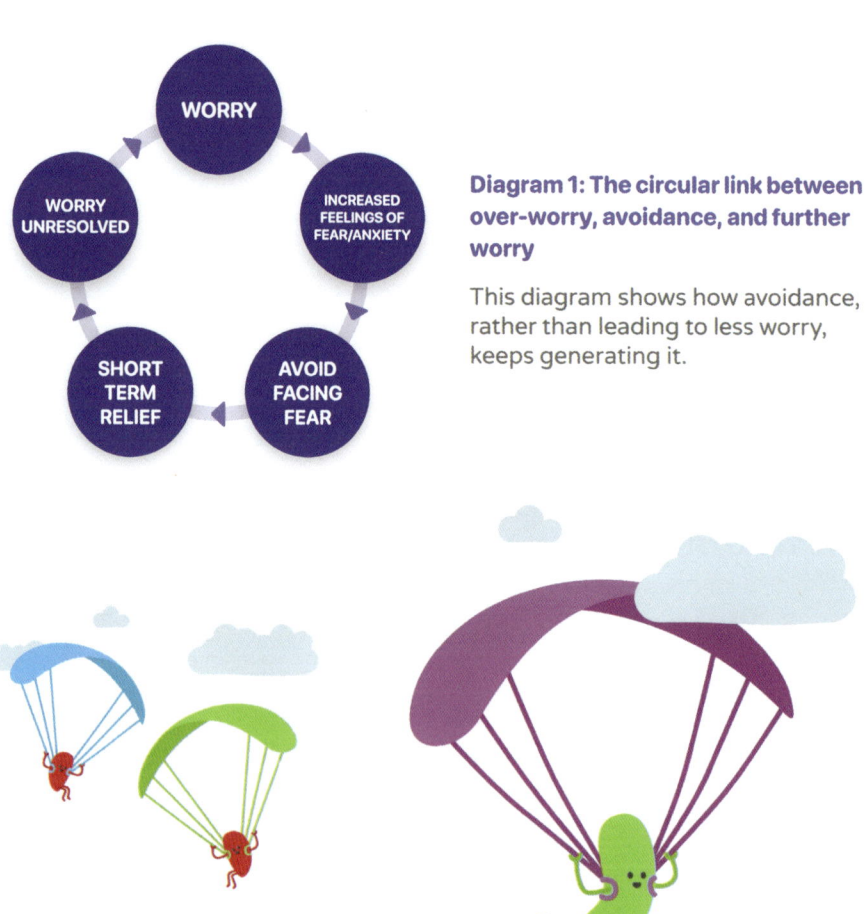

**Diagram 1: The circular link between over-worry, avoidance, and further worry**

This diagram shows how avoidance, rather than leading to less worry, keeps generating it.

**Diagram 2: The negative circle of avoidance**

Although, as diagram 1 shows avoidance might bring about short term relief, missing school in the long term creates other stresses that make returning back even harder. Help for the treatment of Emotional Based School Avoidance (EBDA) therefore focusses on helping a young person face what they fear, as well as support what they may have missed out.

### What help will usually focus on:

1. Identifying worries so that steps can be taken to change whatever needs changing in real life.
2. Learning to reduce the body tension that increases with worry and feeds into the anxiety response.
3. Breathing in special ways to reduce anxiety.
4. Dealing with worries by changing the way you think.
5. Not letting worries take hold—noticing them and just letting them float away or putting them away to deal with at a different time.
6. Letting in other emotions (like laughter) to make the worries smaller and more manageable.
7. Rather than avoiding, learning to face what you fear, going into school or college, one step at a time.
8. Noticing all the things that are positive in a happy journal.

# SOME QUICK AND EFFECTIVE TIPS TO HELP YOUNG PEOPLE LEARN TO MANAGE THEIR WORRIES AND FEARS

The Clear Fear app is a helpful companion to manage anxiety since it provides ideas for young people on how to feel less worried, to reduce body tension, and to face what they are finding difficult to face, one step at a time. The app uses an effective treatment approach called Cognitive Behavioural Therapy or CBT.

## 1. Follow the breathing activity on the Clear Fear app if you have it

In this breathing activity, breathe in as the dot gets bigger and breathe out as the dot gets smaller.

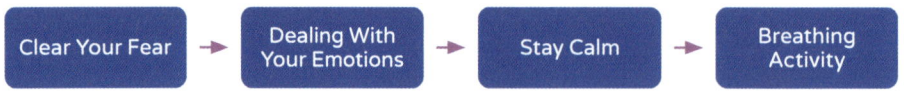

**If you don't have the app**
Try 'Take5 Breathing' - Scan the QR code and watch the video.

1. Put your hand out with your fingers outstretched.

2. Take the finger of your other hand and trace the outside of your thumb and breathe in.

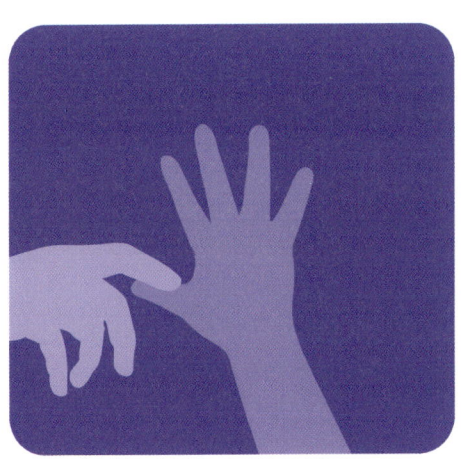

3. Now trace the inside of your thumb and breathe out.

4. Do the same for each of your fingers until you get to the outside of your little finger.

## 2. Have a break from worrying

### Try a mindfulness exercise

Choose one of the calm scenes and just notice.

If you have a worry about school pop into your head while you're watching one of scenes, just let the worry float away and keep watching the calm scene.

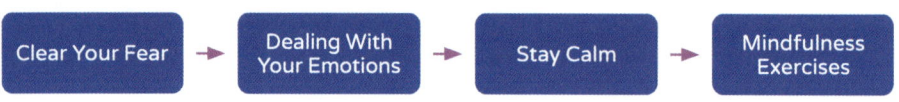

**If you don't have the app**

Focus on your senses:

- What can you hear?
- What can you see?
- What can you touch?
- What can you smell?
- What can you taste?

Keep noticing…

**Make a list of what to do to manage the physical symptoms of worry and anxiety**

*For example, first I will do my Take5 breathing, then I will focus on my senses.*

## Laugh and smile

Have a little laugh by having a look at the jokes and GIFs in the laugh and smile section of the Clear Fear app. It helps to stop worrying all the time and to focus on something nice.

## Use a 'Worry Box'

Here you can write your worries, put them in the 'Worry Box', and either get rid of them or just deal with them at another time.

If you don't have the Clear Fear app you can also write a list of your worries and keep them aside so you can face your step for the day. Tear up the list once you've done your step for the day.

### If you don't have the Clear Fear app
*Write a list of your worries and keep them aside so you can face your step for the day. Tear up the list once you've done your step for the day.*

### Use a 'Worry Ladder'

You can use a 'Worry Ladder' to put your worries in order from smallest to largest and then try and just focus on one at a time.

**Draw your worry ladder here**

Place your smallest worry at the bottom and your biggest worry at the top.

**Now, 'think small and then, when you've done this, think even smaller'.** So, if your smallest worry is the thought of the journey to school, thinking smaller might be a thought of going to your front door. Thinking even smaller might be leaving your room.

Now, focus on the smallest worry, remind yourself that this is a tiny worry and that before it there are no worries. Focus on what it feels like to have no worries.

Use what the no worry looks like to you to think about the smallest worry. See how small it is, breathe and focus on the next small worry.

Remember, if you feel overwhelmed, you are thinking too big. Think small and shrink the worry, it works!

## Change your worry thoughts

The Worry Warriors can help you change some of your worry thoughts—ask an adult to help you.

## 3. Still feeling tense? Manage your physical response to anxiety

There are also things you can do if your body is all tense or your heart is racing.

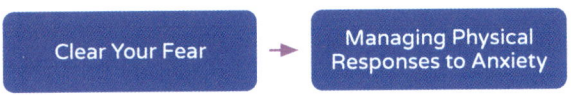

A. **Do something active or some exercise**

For example, do some jogging, star jumps, play with a football, or dance.

B. **Do something relaxing**

Or you can do the opposite and try and feel as relaxed and calm as you can be. The 'Make Time To Relax' section gives ideas of things you can do, or you can write your own. For example, sit somewhere quiet or put on your favourite music.

Once you have a handle on reducing body tension and managing anxious thoughts, it's important to break the cycle of avoidance.

## 4. Make an action plan with small steps

Now you are ready to put together an action plan to getting to school/college.

The '**Reacting To Worries**' section helps you to face your fear by facing going to school or college one small step at a time.

You will feel fearful but breathe, tense, then relax. Look at the next step you must make, and you will be able to get there.

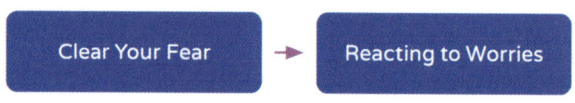

**An example action plan might be:**

1. The evening before I go to school/college, make the journey to school with a parent so that I can get used to the journey.
2. Get up on time.
3. Get ready on time.
4. Leave with someone who makes me feel safe by 8am.
5. Do my breathing exercises whilst I travel to school.
6. Plan who I go into school/college with.
7. Know which classroom my first lesson is in.
8. Get started on my first lesson.
9. Keep breathing throughout the lesson.
10. Make the first half of the day work.
11. Then make the second half work.

And finally, it's important to build your confidence.

## My action plan

*Write what you are going to do to go back to school or college, one small step at a time. Write your smallest step at the bottom of the ladder, your biggest step at the top of the ladder.*

*Remember: If you do something small, you can do even smaller. So, if the smallest thing to do is getting dressed for school or college, thinking smaller might be getting out of bed. Thinking even smaller might be opening your eyes when the alarm goes.*

*Now, do the smallest action. Remind yourself that this is within your control.*

*Proceed onto the next smallest action.*

*Remember, if you can't do it, you have jumped too many steps ahead.*

*Take small steps, they work!*

## 5. Keep a happy journal

You can also keep a journal to remind yourself of things that make life nice. Or you can keep your own private, happy diary.

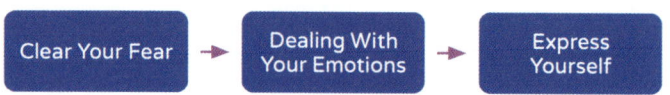

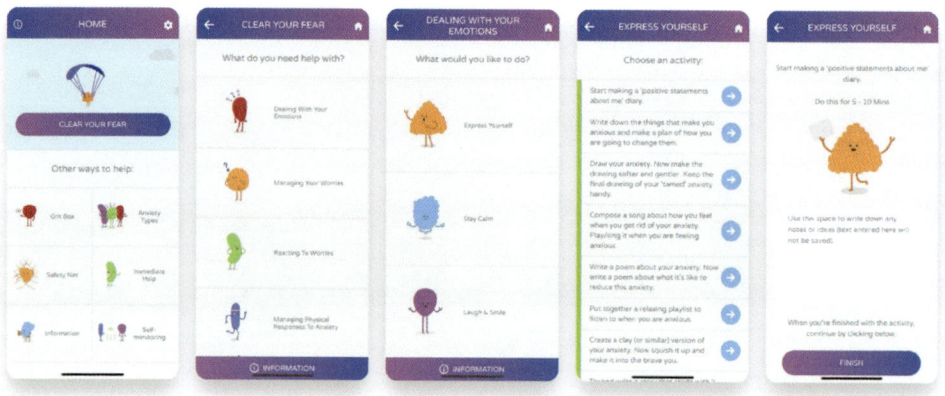

**Some things you can write include:**

- What you have in your life now that you appreciate and like
- Nice things that people say / have said about you
- All the relaxing feelings you get when you do something you enjoy
- People you admire (you can also read some inspirational statement in the 'Grit Box' section of the app)
- Your favourite things

## 6. Try Dr Krause's toothbrush thought exercise

**When you brush your teeth in the morning, think of one positive thing about yourself and how you might put it into practice that day.**

For example, *'I like that I'm smiley.'*

Then, make sure you smile to at least three people in the day and notice what happens.

When you brush your teeth at night remind yourself of the positive thing you did.

For example, *'When I smiled, someone smiled back at me and waved too. I like being a smiley person.'*

**Notes:**

**Notes:**

# WISE WORDS ON SCHOOL/COLLEGE WORRY

Worry always has a start and a finish. Learn to identify what gets it started, how to manage it, and it will finish.

Worry starts in how we think but makes our bodies go tense. By relaxing body tension through activity, exercise, breathing, thinking other non-worry thoughts, worry reduces.

Worry is always the worst before an event. Once you are there, it dies down. So, if your worry is about going to school or college, it will feel the worst before you get there. This is called 'anticipatory anxiety'.

To help with anticipatory anxiety, distract yourself, calm yourself, keep yourself active and busy in the time before. This will make it easier.

Worry makes us fearful, and fear makes us want to run away or avoid. Face fear one small step at a time. This means deciding you will go to school or college, but that you will first get through:

- Step 1. Getting up
- Step 2. Getting dressed
- Step 3. Having breakfast
- Step 4. Keeping your mind busy and your body calm
- Step 5. Getting there
- Step 6. Settling

## PARENTS AND CARERS

Your help in each and all the practical ways outlined above is essential.

Please note the reasons for the worries on Exercise 1, if they are shared with you, and take suitable steps to make changes, especially if they require adult support in terms of: family change; getting some extra help (e.g., catching up on school/college work, counselling); helping to address friendship, relationship, or growing up needs.

Whilst more extensive information is provided for parents and carers in the accompanying booklet here are some basic steps in the support you can offer:

1. Listen to your child or young person's worries and show them you want to understand the blocks to their difficulties in attending school or college.

2. Get their permission on approaching school or college with the difficulties.

3. Inform the school or college as soon as possible, and work together on creating a support plan.

4. Research indicates that the sooner a plan can be drawn up the easier it is to break anxiety behaviours.

Involve your child or young person as much in the plan as possible. As the saying goes *'You can take a horse to water, but you can't make it drink'.*

5. Follow Dr Krause's '3 P' approach to management – be positive, patient and pro-active. Change takes consistency and time.

6. Search for support for yourself. It is extremely upsetting and draining as a parent, especially since it might make you feel helpless or as though you are being blamed for not getting it right. It is also upsetting to see your young person struggling. Anxiety is a mental health condition. It isn't your young person's or your fault.

## Some Troubleshooting Tips

### What do I do if my child or young person just doesn't want to be involved?

Hold in mind that the reason they don't want to be involved is because they feel helpless or powerlessness rather than because they are 'being difficult.' Try and engage them to do something else that they will get involved in and work on building some rapport with them.

Keep updating them on the plan even if they don't want to join in discussions. You can always provide them with some multiple choice answers.

### What do I do if my child or young person wants to carry out the plan, but their anxiety is too great, and they just can't?

Anxiety is an overwhelming feeling and not only makes a child or young person feel uncomfortable physically but also freezes them from being able to apply any problem solving strategies. Help them to reduce the physical feelings through breathing, activity etc. as outlined and then work on 'thinking small and smaller.'

Try not to lose your cool. Getting angry will just make them feel even more helpless. You wouldn't shout at a terrified child, it's just that their fear isn't visible.

**What do I do with myself when I feel so helpless?**

Apply some of the calming strategies to yourself. Be clear, calm, use 'I' sentences and provide positive reinforcement. Keep instructions short:

- *"I want you to get out of bed." "I will come back in five minutes to help with the next step".*
- Then leave the room and come back.
- If they are not out of bed, then say, *"I can either give you five minutes to get out of bed or I can help you to get out of bed so you can try the next small step on your own".*
- Keep facilitating small steps to change until they are able to proceed to the next step.
- Keep helping with managing big emotions but providing strategies to help calm.
- Provide 'growth' feedback. This means providing with the reasons for why they have succeeded.
- *"I can see you managed to get out of bed because you said you were determined to and made a promise to yourself last night, well done for meeting your commitment".*

**Should I take them out of school or college?**

It might be tempting to move them to another school or college. However, facing a new change when they are anxious is likely to make them even more anxious. Work on helping them get their confidence back by getting back on track and then calmly explore your options together.

## SCHOOLS AND COLLEGES

There is a 'triangle of change' which involves the young person, parents/carers and school/college as the three arms that needs balancing in order for a successful programme to help manage EBSA.

From the point of view of school/college, it makes sense to be involved to best support the young person to return to school/college, to be involved in showing care so that the young person feels important and welcomed back, to help minimise lost learning, to keep social connections intact and to help with resourcing. EBSA is a lonely condition, so building and maintaining caring connections goes a long way.

With regards resourcing, to have an effective prevention strategy in place to support a young person to remain in school/college, compared to getting a young person back into school/college after a long absence which requires a substantial investment of resource – both in time and money.

Here are some of the supports that young people tell us would have, or can help:

- Safe space to go at breaks and lunchtimes.
- Time out cards and clear instructions on how to use them.
- Supporting parents/carers in getting the young person into school/college - provide a place for them to calm down before starting classes.
- Staggered starts
- Group interventions with other young people in breaks lunchtimes/lessons struggling with friendships and communication, setting group tasks to practice skills.
- Listening to parents and young people's concerns and providing solutions to problems.

Schools and colleges can help by looking at the reasons in Exercise 1 in terms of what the positives of the school or college are for the young person and what would make school or college a less worrying place. This requires discretion and a problem-solving approach to any difficulties that might be contributing to the EBSA. Examples may include; extra maths help, or inclusion in a new social group or a lunchtime responsibility to help manage difficulty of going into the canteen when feeling anxious.

Anxiety needs a graded, phased-in approach with the young person, parents/carers, and school or college all working together to help achieve the goal of getting back to school or college one small step at a time.

**A graded approach has been derived from Behavioural Therapy. It is comprised of continual goals of increasing difficulty until the final goal can be achieved.**

**The theory behind it indicates that being exposed to a hierarchy of fear, helps overcome anxiety. This approach targets avoidance behaviours and works on a process called habituation, which is a noted gradual decrease in the physical sensations of anxiety through practice.**

There are four principles of a graded approach – the first that it needs to be a stepped approach, that it needs a specific focus, it has to happen over time in order for habituation to occur and that it needs to be repeated in order to master fear.

The first two steps are the ones that need the most attention and that need to be broken into very small achievable steps. Learning through confidence building and scaffolding is a well-known strategy in teaching and one that all educators will be familiar with.

Graded approaches are applied on the assumption that there are no major difficulties that need treating either alongside or first. Certain conditions such as trauma, for example, will need robust treatment first. Neurodevelopmental conditions such as Attention Deficit Hyperactivity Disorder (ADHD) or Autism Spectrum Disorder (ASD) will need diagnosis and relevant support, for example, to deal with sensory sensitivity to ensure the graded approach is individualised to support the young person.

More about how to support these conditions can be accessed by contacting your school or college Special Educational Needs Coordinator, the local Special Educational Needs and Disability Service or the Child and Adolescent Mental Health Service (CAMHS).

# ABOUT STEM4

## Who we are

stem4 is a charity that promotes positive mental health in teenagers and those who support them including their families, carers, and education professionals, as well as school nurses and GPs, through the provision of mental health education, resilience strategies, and early intervention.

This is primarily provided digitally through our innovative education programme, pioneering mental health apps, clinically-informed website, and mental health conferences that contribute to helping young people and those around them flourish.

## Dr Nihara Krause MBE
Consultant Clinical Psychologist, CEO and Founder of stem4

Dr. Nihara Krause founded stem4 based on the knowledge that early identification and intervention made a real difference in stemming what has recently been reported to be escalating teenage mental health conditions in their often serious and long-lasting course.

Nihara has many years of clinical experience working in a variety of mental health settings with both young people and adults. She has specialist experience in eating disorders and self-harm. Nihara is also a university lecturer, works extensively with the media, and has input in informing government on youth matters. She has a special interest in building resilience, as well as practicing effective treatment techniques for a variety of psychological problems. Nihara is the clinician who developed the award-winning Calm Harm, Clear Fear, Move Mood, and Combined Minds apps for stem4.

Most recently, Nihara developed the Worth Warrior app, stem4's latest app which helps manage low self-worth and body dissatisfaction leading to eating difficulties.

## CLEAR FEAR

The fear of threat, or anxiety, is like a strong gust of wind. It drags you in and makes you want to fight it or run away.

Instead, face your fear with the free Clear Fear app and learn to reduce the physical responses to threat as well as changing thoughts and behaviours and releasing emotions.

Anxiety is a natural response to fear, threat and apprehension. However, when anxiety is extreme or goes on for a long time, or the response to a threat is disproportionately large and affects a person negatively, it may become an anxiety disorder.

Anxiety disorders are the most common form of emotional disorder and respond very well to a form of treatment called Cognitive Behavioural Therapy or CBT.

When you face your fear, you will reduce the threat and glide.

www.clearfear.co.uk
@clearfearapp

Please note that none of the stem4 apps substitute for seeing a mental health professional / GP. Please see a suitably qualified professional for assessment and advice on treatment.

# STEM4'S MENTAL HEALTH APPS

### CALM HARM
A free app to help teenagers resist or manage the urge to self-harm

www.calmharm.co.uk
@calmharmapp

### CLEAR FEAR
A free app to help children and young people manage the symptoms of anxiety

www.clearfear.co.uk
@clearfearapp

### COMBINED MINDS
A free app to help families and friends provide mental health support

www.combinedminds.co.uk
@combmindsapp

### MOVE MOOD
A free app to help young people manage the behaviours associated with low mood or depression

www.movemood.co.uk
@appmovemood

### WORTH WARRIOR
A free app to help young people manage negative body image, poor self-worth, and related early-stage eating difficulties or disorders

www.worthwarrior.co.uk
@worthwarriorapp

stem4's award-winning apps are available to download from the App Store and Google Play.

 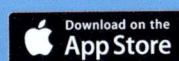

Please note that these apps are an aid in treatment but do not replace it.

www.stem4.org.uk • @stem4org

Developed by stem4 • Registered Charity No. 1144506

# SIGNPOSTS FOR YOUNG PEOPLE

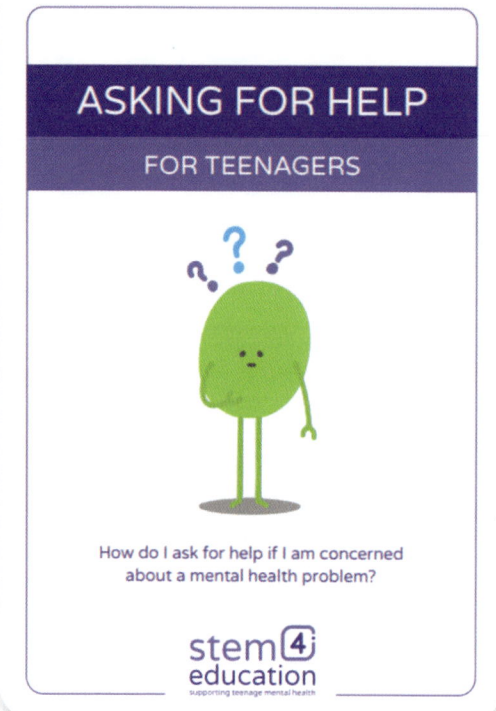

Follow this QR code to view the **stem4 asking for help** booklet

1. If you are worried, please speak to a trusted adult such as someone from your family, school or ask to see a doctor who can help.
2. Some schools will have counsellors or adults who can help.
3. There are some helplines, but they are all generally for teenagers or adults.
    - Childline **0800 111** will answer calls to anyone of any age.
    - SHOUT - you can text **SHOUT** to **85258**

# SIGNPOSTS FOR ADULTS

stem4 offers a wide range of resources to help parents and carers support their young people:

Our website has detailed information to help you support a young person experiencing anxiety, stress and a variety of other mental ill health conditions.
www.stem4.org.uk

Our podcast 'Understanding Teen Minds podcast, episode on Emotionally Based School Avoidance Podcast for teachers
www. stem4.org.uk/podcasts

Our resources - stem4 has a wealth of resources that can be accessed online. They are designed with young people and combine the clinical expertise of a Consultant Clinical Psychologist with the needs expressed by our young people.

Links to all our Anxiety apps, resources and podcasts can be accessed via our link tree using the QR code here.

For more information visit stem4.org

Printed in Great Britain
by Amazon